Periphrasis; or the Art of Circumlocution

Poems by

Pamela Martin

Periphrasis; or the Art of Circumlocution
Copyright 2009 by Pamela Gowan

All rights reserved under International and Pan-American copyright conventions. No part of this book may be reproduced, stored in a retrieval system or transmitted in any form, electronic, mechanical, or by any other means, without written permission of the author.

International Standard Book Number: 978-0-578-01509-5

Illustrated by Kathleen Hardy.

Table of Contents
Part I

Performance Anxiety	9
P.A.M., My Heroine	9
Fool's Gold	9
The Blahs	10
"In Praise of Folly"	10
Poetry	10
The Feminine Mystique	11
Mary Poppins?	12
A Nuclear Holocaust	12
"Doubting Thomas"	12
The Handy Man	13
"A Fine Disregard"	14
Time Passages	14
Fatigue	14
"Rhombi Are Forever"	15
The Manicure	16
One Day	16
To and Fro	16
"Searching for the Soul within the Body" or "Soul Searching?"	17
Miracle Workers	18
Gathering Rosebuds	18
The Mystery of History	18
Avoidance	19
From Manic to Panic	20
Soulful	20
Wear Apparent	20
Sweetest Day	21
He Lives!	21
Lifting My Spirits High!	21
The Loves of My Life	22
A 3/5 Compromise	22
Chronically Dilatory	22
Living by My Wits	23
A Beacon or a Spire?	23
No Good Deed Goes Unpunished	23
Separation Anxiety	24

Part II

"The Roadie" ... 27
Three's Company ... 27
A Threat or a Promise? ... 27
P.T.L. ... 28
The Straw That Broke Pamela's Neck ... 28
Halloween? ... 28
Mindlessness ... 29
Birches or Churches? ... 30
Better or Worse? ... 30
Passing the Hat ... 30
The Hitchhiker's Guide to the Universe ... 31
Exquisite Perquisites ... 32
"I Got a Vocabulary for Christmas" ... 32
Lovely Lucretia ... 32
A Mouse Pudica ... 33
Push and Pull ... 34
Kosher Kats ... 34
Short But Sweet ... 34
Incredulous ... 35
Destination Unknown ... 36
Transubstantiation ... 36
Written in the Stars ... 36
Depraved? ... 37
A Cat Lover ... 38
Civics 101 ... 38
Flippancy ... 38
School Daze ... 39
Dog Tags ... 39
The Compost Heap ... 39
The Ebb and Flow of Life ... 40
"The Pelvis" ... 40
The School of Hard Knocks ... 40
Half *or* Half ... 41
Been There/Done That ... 41
Nocturnal ... 41
Your Boring Snoring ... 42

Part III

Forty Whacks 45
Biscuit Eater 45
Optical Resolution 45
My Mantra 46
Unconditional Love 46
Surprise! 46
Good Advice 46
Preternatural Damnation 47
The Convalescent 48
A Frugality 48
A Vanderbilt 48
The War of Roses 49
Bertro 50
Sustenance 50
A Pandemic 50
180° 51
Mistress Distress 52
In Your Face 52
Christmas in My Heart 52
Simple Simon? 53
Venality 54
Mendacity/Veracity 54
A Free-for-All 54
Decapitated 55
"Worthless and Unworthy" 56
Astray 56
Pick Your Battles 56
Oenology 57
The Internet 57
The Quintessence of Dust 57
The Wrong Song 58
Shocking News 58
An Essential 58
Food Fair 59
"With Bells On" 59
Benumbed 59
Alice 59
Not! 60
James Bondage 60
Shakespearean Rhetoric 60
The Regatta of Life 61

Part I

Performance Anxiety

Did you ever see a square dance
Or a patriot act?
I have seen them with both eyes,
And it is a fact
That neither is edifying
Nor particularly enlightening
But both can be terrifying
And especially frightening.

P.A.M., My Heroine

This is my epic poem
I have written for no one.
Perhaps it would be better
If it were left undone.
But here it is before you.
She is that someone
You don't mind well knowing.
She is so much fun.

Fool's Gold

Well is a deep subject
I delve into all the time.
If I got a penny every time I said it,
I would have a dime.
It doesn't really matter
If what they say is true.
In the end, you always
Played me for a fool.

The Blahs

Blah, blah, blah, blah, blah, blah, blah.
Blah, blah, blah, blah, blah.
Blah, blah, blah, blah, blah, blah, blah.
Blah, blah, blah, blah, blah.
Blah, blah, blah, blah, blah, blah, blah.
Blah, blah, blah.
Blah, blah, blah, blah, blah, blah, blah.
Blah, blah, blah.

"In Praise of Folly"

I'm due for retirement.
I don't know how long
I can write this rubbish.
But I could be wrong.
People will read it
Until the cows come home
As if they have no standards
And no caller I.D. on their phone.

Poetry

My legacy grows larger
With each passing day.
But wouldn't you go figure?
I have nothing to say.
But any way you say it,
I am here to stay.
Today is all that matters.
I will not go away.

The Feminine Mystique

Man created God
In his own image
Replete with bushy eyebrows
And a smiling visage.
He lacked imagination
Because he had no vision.
We could do it better
And with more precision.

Mary Poppins?

I never make mistakes.
One time I was wrong.
I do my best in every way
Just to get along.
I know it would be better
For me to now admit
I am not so perfect
I humbly submit.

A Nuclear Holocaust

I'm as hairy as an ape
In places you don't know.
I cannot escape them.
How quickly they do grow.
Yes, my name is Harry.
I'm a real Truman.
I only blame myself.
But we had to win.

"Doubting Thomas"

"Repetition is needless,"
Is what I always say.
There is something new
Each and every day.
There are those who doubt me.
"Thomas" is their name.
But I doubt even Thomas
Would like that claim to fame.

The Handy Man

Creature comforts are his thing.
He understands most everything
And alleviates all suffering.
He always takes command.
I should know 'cuz I was there
When he made his first repair
Wearing only underwear.
He is the handy man.

"A Fine Disregard"

Sometimes you don't notice
That I'm even there.
But that doesn't mean
That you do not care.
It means there will be times
I will be on my own.
And there will be times
I will be all alone.

Time Passages

The good times are behind me.
They are dead and gone.
I take solace in the knowledge
The memories live on.
The next forty-seven
May not be as good.
But this I know for certain:
I did the best I could.

Fatigue

I did not enjoy
My special two-faced book.
It was too fatiguing
To take a second look.
But it ended nicely
(Or that was the buzz).
It made me so stressed out
Because that's what I was.

"Rhombi Are Forever"

Charging cards is my thing.
I just bought a diamond ring.
Were it so that "cash is king"
I could not buy anything.

The Manicure

My finger nails are
As tough as nails.
They take the wind
Out of my sails.
When I bite,
They bite me back.
It's enough to cause
A heart attack.

One Day

Today I know today is Sunday.
But I know it's not my fun day.
Give to me my manic Monday!
I know that it will be some day.

To and Fro

I'm all dressed up
With no where to go.
The "nowhere man"
Told me so.
Just in case
You didn't know,
You are walking
To and fro.

"Searching for the Soul within the Body" or "Soul Searching?"*

I have periphrasis.
I paraphrase my words.
So much so, I have to say
At times, it sounds absurd.
I want to be periphrastic "meaningfully"+
(It has been a lifelong goal)
But I simply cannot do it
If I want to bare my soul.

*You decide. +I allude here to the Aristotelian concept of the "golden mean."

Miracle Workers

Friends are truly miracles
In this day and age.
Castor and Pollux
Have long exited the stage.
Friends are very special
If what they say is true.
I am very lucky
To have a friend like you.

Gathering Rosebuds

Wise men and sages
Say that it is true:
Freedom only lasts
For a day or two.
Liberty is fleeting.
Enjoy it while you can.
Unless, of course, you discover
You are Peter Pan.

The Mystery of History

The night is young,
And so are we.
We are all
That we can be.
Life is but
A mystery.
The rest, they say,
Is history.

Avoidance

I am just a writer.
I am self-employed.
But deep inside of me
There is such a void.
A void so big
It can't be filled
Although I try
With drink distilled.

From Manic to Panic

The economy is in trouble.
How safe is your bank?
The Federal Reserve
You have to thank
For insuring the money
In your account
So you will have
The same amount.

Soulful

I need a light jacket.
This one is tan.
Without it,
I'd be a man.
Without you,
I would be whole
Although I would have
Lost my soul.

Wear Apparent

I almost forgot
That the dry rot
Does the Fox Trot
In my living room.
If I say so,
It must soon go
Like a good foe
Or family heirloom.

Sweetest Day

My father is a "sweet guy."
He loves all his sweets.
He is on a diet
But he likes his treats.
The doctor always warns him
To eat only meats.
But he smiles and tells him,
"I like sugar beets."

He Lives!*

There's no one like Elvis.
Just look around.
He makes his rivals
Look just like clowns.
They make you laugh.
They make you cry.
But you prefer Elvis.
You don't know why.

*"Lives" is an anagram for "Elvis" as is "evils."

Lifting My Spirits High!

You make me so happy.
I say it every day.
And I try to show it
In each and every way.
The only way to say it
And not give it short shrift
Is to acknowledge
You give me a lift!

The Loves of My Life

I never thought they'd be
So much a part of us.
There's no need to explain
Or even discuss
The meaning of true love.
Once it is found
There is enough
To go around.

A 3/5 Compromise

Touch and sight and sound
Are three of our five senses.
When used properly,
They are good defenses
Against the dangerous inroads
We encounter along the way
From which there is no return
Until Judgment Day.

Chronically Dilatory

Before the fat I looked like that.
My smile was very big.
My hair was thick as a wick.
I did not wear a wig.
But I do now. I don't know how
Or another way to say it.
The past is past. It happens fast.
You can only delay it.

Living by My Wits

If I sometimes sound like me,
What is wrong with that?
Is it true that what I do
Can cause a heart attack?
Any time my simple rhyme
Makes you want to laugh,
Then you know what I have done
Is clever by half.

A Beacon or a Spire?

I have high blood pressure
And high cholesterol.
Caduet may help
Both of them to fall.
If I should tell the story
Of my fall from grace,
You should listen closely
To avoid this loathsome place.

No Good Deed Goes Unpunished

When somebody helps you,
Don't bite him in the ass.
Doing that will only
Make you seem crass.
But we often do it
For his own good
To stop him from doing
All that he could.

Separation Anxiety

We started out so happy.
What went so terribly wrong?
You and me together
Singing our love song.
Now we hardly speak
With each passing day.
Silence is not golden.
Together we can't stay.

Part II

"The Roadie"

"I prefer a road trip to a road kill,"
The wily rodent said.
One is so much fun.
One fills me with such dread.
When the road is winding,
I go with the flow
Because death and dying
I don't want to know.

Three's Company

We are three strong women
Living with one man.
You may not believe it
Or even understand
That living in a harem
Such as we do
Begets a curiosity
More than we want to.

A Threat or a Promise?

If it wasn't for me,
You'd be on your own
Leading a dull life
Hitherto unknown.
But you know I am with you,
With you all the way.
And you know for certain
I am here to stay.

P.T.L.*

I am a television evangelist.
I pray on T.V.
No one is more popular
But I can plainly see
That you do not listen
To a single word I say.
Just keep the money coming.
I have bills to pay.

*"Praise the Lord" syndicate.

The Straw That Broke Pamela's Neck

I am the neck.
You are the head.
I am the butter.
You are the bread.
I use a straw
To drink my coffee hot.
You use a spoon
Or drink from the pot.

Halloween?

I wear a mask throughout the year.
But I must admit
It fills me with such aching fear
That I do not permit
Anyone to take it off
Lest somebody should see
That what I'm hiding is quite real,
The all too sensitive me.

Mindlessness

If the cats play while we're away,
I say then so-be-it.
I don't care what they dare
As long as I don't see it.

Birches or Churches?

The minister always guilts me
When I go to church.
I tell myself every day
I prefer a birch.
Robert Frost said it best
Is all that I can say.
I'd rather be a swinger than a choir singer
On Sunday.

Better or Worse?

I've been better
And I've been worse.
Better is better
And worse is worse.
I've been rich
And I've been poor.
It is something
You can't ignore.

Passing the Hat

Tithing is a way
To pay God off.
I have to say in my own way
It makes me want to cough
When I see the coffers
Opening up.
But it is the cheapest way
To buy good luck.

The Hitchhiker's Guide to the Universe

I ran out of money.
I thought it was funny.
And it was sunny
In Newport that day.
So, I stuck out my thumb
(I know it was dumb)
But it was fun
I now can safely say.

Exquisite Perquisites

The ballet has spoiled me.
But I could not stay
In a box so high.
I ran away.
I love dance and music
And a glass of wine
But to me the Atwood
Is far too sublime.

"I Got a Vocabulary for Christmas"

A "juggernaut" is
An irrepressible force
Used to denote
A going off course.
I use it glibly
But I don't really know
What a juggernaut is.
I hope it don't show.

Lovely Lucretia

You're the guilty pleasure
I can't resist.
Never could there ever
Be one who exists
Purer than pure,
Truer than blue.
You know who
I'm talking to.

A Mouse Pudica*

There's a mouse in the house.
I want her out.
It makes me so mad
I want to shout!
I know it is her
Because she runs away
Whenever the cats
Come out to play.

*A "shy" mouse.

Push and Pull

You're pulling my leg.
You're pulling my chain.
You're pulling at something
I can't explain.
You're pushing my buttons.
You're pushing the muck.
You're pushing the envelope.
You're pushing your luck.

Kosher Kats

Gravy is groovy to Tabby.
Pate is precious to Sam.
Either way you slice it,
It is better than ham.

Short But Sweet

Is there a better time?
Is the question of the day.
I don't have an answer
Is all I can say.
"Carpe diem"
I often repeat.
But I know in my heart
We'll never meet.

Incredulous

Nothing is real.
Nothing at all.
But I still pray
To Sts. Peter and Paul.
Things aren't what they used to be.
Maybe *you* know.
But I don't know what to think
Or where I should go.

Destination Unknown

If the train is late you have to wait
Until it comes along
Or until you find you're celibate
But won't be for long.
Don't despair just pay the fare.
Today is the day
To celebrate and seal your fate.
You are on your way.

Transubstantiation

Sometimes mamma goes
To the ballet dance
Where she leads a life
Of magic and romance.
But when it's all over
She's well aware
The life she knows
Cannot compare.

Written in the Stars

I may not be a writer.
It might be untrue.
But it is what I say
And it is what I do.
You have within your grasp
All the proof you need
To help you understand
This is the life I lead.

Depraved?

I'm not the best at what I do
But I do it just the same.
If you tried it, you would know
Exactly who's to blame
For too much introspection
And too much levity
And too much degradation
And depravity.

A Cat Lover

My cats are adorable.
That's why I love them so.
They wiggle and connive
Until I let them go.
When they are not sleeping
(Which is all the time)
I truly am convinced
They are part divine.

Civics 101

I have a 'B' mind
If I mind at all.
That's better than nothing.
At least I recall
Who ran for office
And who won the race.
To fail at this
Would mean disgrace.

Flippancy

Flip the light.
Flip the bird.
Flip this house
And be abjured.
Flip out over nothing.
Flip out over her.
Flip out over the carpets
And the furniture.

School Daze

A school of thought.
A school of fish.
A school that does not
Have a niche.
A school for scandal.
A school for rhyme.
A school that does not
Cost a dime.

Dog Tags

The collar makes the cat
As tame as she can be.
Without it she's more
Like a mystery.
What is her name?
Where does she live?
I cannot be
More positive.

The Compost Heap

Organic waste
Should be thrown away
In a receptacle
Where it can stay
Until it is picked up
Every day
Or until it's recycled
In a soufflé.

The Ebb and Flow of Life

I found out the hard way
When I was a kid
What matters most
Is what you did.
It will haunt you
Wherever you go
And will totally drown you
In the undertow.

"The Pelvis"

I went to Graceland
On a pilgrimage
To worship his shrine
And pay homage.
He lived a wild life
As many would say.
But I miss my dear Elvis
More every day.

The School of Hard Knocks

What little I learned,
I learned in school:
Never break
The Golden Rule.
Because in the end
It comes back to you.
And, when it does,
You are a fool.

Half *or* Half

Half-naked or half-dressed
Depends solely on you
And who it is
You're talking to.
Parading around
Like a peacock
Only leads
To culture shock.

Been There/Done That

You're not an original.
No, far from it.
They say your good fortune
Will eventually plummet
If you don't reach
That high summit.
Take it from someone
Who has been there and done it.

Nocturnal

When you rest,
You rest at night
Unless you sleep
In broad daylight.
Day is day
All day long.
But night is where
We belong.

Your Boring Snoring

When you do something every day,
It gets monotonous and boring.
But what afflicts me more and more
Is your sonorous snoring.

Part III

Forty Whacks

Liberation is an ax.
Cliches are for writing hacks.
Wolves travel in large packs
And so do we.
You stopped dead in your tracks.
Stick to the salient facts.
Smoke comes from dirty stacks.
Kindly let me be.

Biscuit Eater

Have some coffee.
It works for me.
Some coffee and biscuits
And steaming, hot tea
Get me up in the morning
And move me along.
It can work wonders
But I could be wrong.

Optical Resolution

I'm looking at you.
You're looking at me.
We ogle each other
So tenderly.
But when you look,
What do you see?
I don't think
You see me.

My Mantra

Tolerance and love
Go hand in hand
I have come
To understand.

Unconditional Love

She has a sandpaper tongue
As rough as can be
But I love her
Unconditionally.

Surprise!

If you're everything to everyone,
You're nothing to no one.

Good Advice

"In order to kill time,
Work it to death,"
My father told me
In his final breath.
When advice is not taken
(Although it is free),
You'll be mistaken
Regrettably.

Preternatural Damnation

I empathize and sympathize
With everything you do.
I do my best to give you rest
But I am subject to
The laws of pomp and circumstance.
I know them all too well.
And I can look you in the eye
And send you straight to hell.

The Convalescent

I must harness all my energy
If I'm to win the race.
And I must try in every way
To keep a steady pace.
If I do I say to you,
You must acquiesce
And stand with pride by my side
As I convalesce.

A Frugality

You smell like a factory
That reeks of cheap perfume.
What you say to me presently
Really makes me fume.
To say that it upsets me
Is to say the least.
Understatement in this case
Is a poor man's feast.

A Vanderbilt

Anderson Cooper is a news gnome
We see on T.V.
But he is not a master
Of verbal repartee.
He is the son of money
Who doesn't have to work.
He only serenades us
So he doesn't go berserk.

The War of Roses

We have an English garden
That grows as wild as rice.
Not a topiary.
It isn't quite as nice.
The French manicure their spaces
To the "nth" degree.
Laid back are the English
Like a cup of tea.

Bertro*

Bertro is an anagram
I like quite a lot.
Betro and an ampersand
Make a lovely knot.
It isn't all that common
For me to call him thus
But I gladly do it
To escape from all the fuss.

*"Bertro" is an anagram for Robert.

Sustenance

Raw food.
Cooked food.
Breakfast, lunch,
And dinner food.
Frozen food.
Fresh food.
Everyone loves
Good food.

A Pandemic

I opened the window
And in flu "enza."
That was the day
I joined Mensa.
But I told
The orderly
Just to let
The window be.

180°

Look up. Look down.
Look all around.
A frown is a smile
Upside down.
So turn your frown
Into a smile
And always go
That extra mile.

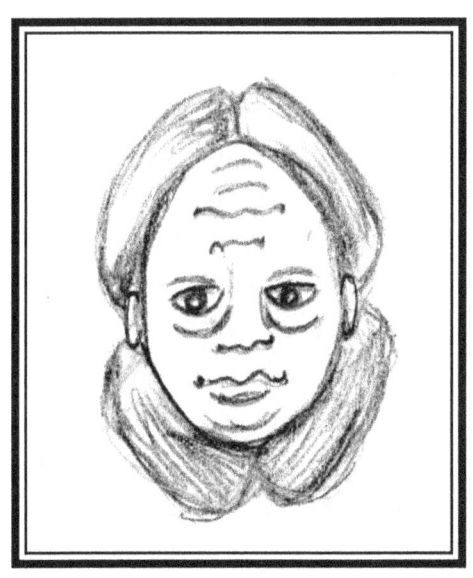

Mistress Distress

I offend many
And please a few.
But what am I
Supposed to do?
When I look left,
The right will sneer.
When I'm in front,
I fear the rear.

In Your Face

I'm the opening act
And the main event.
Now I am paying
All of the rent.
It took a while
To reach this place
Which is why
I'm in your face.

Christmas in My Heart

I have Christmas in my heart
Most of the year.
But there are times
I do fear
I have it not.
It goes away.
And then it's just
Another day.

Simple Simon?

Sometimes I catch the train.
Sometimes it catches me.
What would I do
If I could only see
Tomorrow as today?
Would I carry on
As if I didn't know
Like a simpleton?

Venality

I don't cry in my beer.
I prefer champagne
For obvious reasons
I need not explain.
Champagne is better
When it is fresh.
I know I am going
The way of all flesh.

Mendacity/Veracity

You know what I told.
I told you I lied.
Now it's up to you
To finally decide
What is the truth
And what is a lie,
What to believe
And what to deny.

A Free-for-All

I live in Chicago
On the South side
It is a place
Where you run and hide.
Chicago falls so freely
For everyone to see.
The happening life mayor
Is just the referee.

Decapitated

You can't live with it. You can't live without it.
You have dropped the ball.
You're dead to the world
When you don't give your all.
If someone tells you differently,
Tell them that I said,
"I know from experience.
Use your pretty head."

"Worthless and Unworthy"*

Worthless and unworthy,
I go through the days
Hoping this feeling
Is only a phase.
It visits me sometimes
But it never stays.
It hovers above me
Like a light haze.

Astray

Your mamma and your daddy
Love you more each day.
They take time to tell you
You are not a stray.
But it seems you have gone
And lost your way again.
If we ever find you,
What will you do then?

Pick Your Battles

I tried to help you.
But you cannot count.
With little education,
You would probably amount
To little or nothing.
You may be right.
I was quite wrong
To take up this fight.

Oenology*

"Fermentation" is the heart
Of writing and revision.
And it is an integral part
Of verbal recognition.
Since the past will not last,
We must relive it.
All of those who do oppose
Must learn to forgive it.

*The study of wines and winemaking.

The Internet

In and out
1-2-3.
I check my facts
So easily.
Without you,
I'd be lost
But, God knows,
At what cost.

The Quintessence of Dust

I had a noble impulse
That I have no more.
I come from a place
Where the folks are poor.
But I have more wealth than those
Who have quite a lot
Because I know that I am real
And that time is not.

The Wrong Song

I don't know where I'll be.
I don't know where I've been.
But I know I'm with you now
Although it is a sin.
I do it anyway.
I know it is wrong.
I do it just the same.
I sing right along.

Shocking News

Don't cut your hair.
Lower your ears.
That way you will
Shed those tears,
Those tears of sorrow
When you see
That your hair grows
Fitfully.

An Essential

I do for you.
You do for me.
We do for each other
So selflessly.
Doing unto others
As they do unto you
Is the essence of
The Golden Rule.

Food Fair

Hospital food is terrible.
It cannot compare
To your homestyle favorites.
It makes you aware
That you are not homebound,
That you are not well.
Whatever it is,
Boy, does it smell.

"With Bells On"

Tabby needs a collar.
Her collar needs a bell.
So, wherever Tabby goes
We can always tell.

Benumbed

Numbness comes and numbness goes.
There are times when I suppose
Some day when I'm in repose
I will not be predisposed.

Alice

If I had anything nice to say,
It would not be true.
If I had anything nice to say,
It would not be about you.

Not!

You sound like you.
I sound like me.
We sound like people
Who cannot be.
We're out of sight.
We're out of mind.
We're out of luck.
We're out of time.

James Bondage

Bond is back.
Watch your back
Unless you want
A heart attack.
If you do,
Then good for you.
If you don't,
Watch pay-per-view.

Shakespearean Rhetoric

If it was meant to be,
It was meant to be.
If it has to be,
It has to be.
To be or not to be?
Only begs the question
And causes inside most of us
The greatest indigestion.

The Regatta of Life

I loved him, and he loved me.
We were all that we could be.
But he up and died on me.
We once rowed so merrily.

www.ingramcontent.com/pod-product-compliance
Lightning Source LLC
LaVergne TN
LVHW011430080426
835512LV00005B/371